W9-BXY-224

Lucky Ladybugs

Mary Elizabeth Salzmann

Consulting Editor, Diane Craig, M.A./Reading Specialist

A Division of ABDO

ABDO
Publishing Company

visit us at www.abdopublishing.com

Published by ABDO Publishing Company, a division of ABDO, P.O. Box 398166, Minneapolis, Minnesota 55439. Copyright © 2012 by Abdo Consulting Group, Inc. International copyrights reserved in all countries. No part of this book may be reproduced in any form without written permission from the publisher. SandCastle™ is a trademark and logo of ABDO Publishing Company.

Printed in the United States of America, North Mankato, Minnesota
102011
012012

E

PRINTED ON RECYCLED PAPER   *595.769*
Sal

Editor: Katherine Hengel
Content Developer: Nancy Tuminelly
Cover and Interior Design and Production: Kelly Doudna, Mighty Media, Inc.
Photo Credit: Shutterstock

Library of Congress Cataloging-in-Publication Data

Salzmann, Mary Elizabeth, 1968-
 Lucky ladybugs / Mary Elizabeth Salzmann.
   p. cm. -- (Bug books)
 ISBN 978-1-61783-192-8
 1. Ladybugs--Juvenile literature. I. Title.
 QL596.C65S25 2012
 595.76'9--dc23
                          2011023467

SandCastle™ Level: Transitional

SandCastle™ books are created by a team of professional educators, reading specialists, and content developers around five essential components—phonemic awareness, phonics, vocabulary, text comprehension, and fluency—to assist young readers as they develop reading skills and strategies and increase their general knowledge. All books are written, reviewed, and leveled for guided reading, early reading intervention, and Accelerated Reader® programs for use in shared, guided, and independent reading and writing activities to support a balanced approach to literacy instruction. The SandCastle™ series has four levels that correspond to early literacy development. The levels are provided to help teachers and parents select appropriate books for young readers.

Emerging Readers
(no flags)

Beginning Readers
(1 flag)

Transitional Readers
(2 flags)

Fluent Readers
(3 flags)

Contents

Lucky Ladybugs

Ladybugs are also called ladybirds and lady beetles. Many people think ladybugs are a sign of good luck.

Ladybugs are small and round. They are less than ½ inch (1.25 cm) long.

Ladybugs are red, orange, or yellow. Most ladybugs have black spots.

Ladybugs have hard **outer** wings. They cover the ladybug's body.

Ladybugs also have thin wings. They are under the hard wings. Ladybugs use the thin wings to fly.

Ladybugs have black heads. They have white spots on their faces. Ladybugs have two **antennae**.

Ladybugs can pull their heads in. They do this when they rest.

Ladybugs eat **tiny insects** called **aphids**.

Ladybugs spend the winter in large groups.

Find the Ladybug

A

B

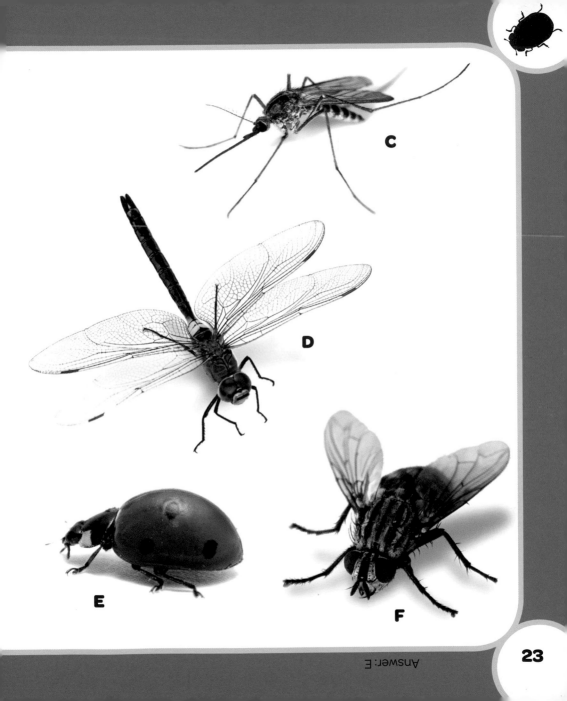

C

D

E

F

Glossary

antenna – a feeler on an insect's head.

aphid – a small insect that eats plant sap.

insect – a small creature with two or four wings, six legs, and a body with three sections.

outer – on the outside.

tiny – very small.